NIGHT TRAIN

NIGHT TRAIN

ANTHONY LYNCH

Clouds of Magellan | Melbourne

© 2011 Anthony Lynch
First published 2011
Clouds of Magellan
www.cloudsofmagellan.net
Melbourne, Australia

ISBN 9780980712087

A Cataloguing-in-Publication record from the National Library of Australia is available for this title

Cover design and layout: Gordon Thompson

Acknowledgements

Poems in this collection previously appeared, sometimes in different form, in *The Age*, *Antipodes* (USA), *Artlook*, *The Best Australian Poems 2004*, *The Best Australian Poems 2010*, *The Best Australian Poems 2011*, *Blue Dog: Australian Poetry*, *A Book of Evidence*, *Egg*, *Island*, *Ekleksographia* (USA), *Eureka Street*, *foam:e*, *Groundwork*, *LiNQ*, *Magma* (UK), *Quadrant*, *Reactions* (UK), *Saltlick: New Poetry*, *Saltlick Quarterly*, *Southerly*, *Stand* (UK), *Tamba*, *Westerly*. Thanks to the editors of these publications.

Thanks also to Cameron Lowe, David McCooey, Kevin Densley and Brendan Ryan, all of whom gave valuable advice on these poems, and to Amanda Frances Johnson, my closest reader, who knows when to take out the trills.

Finally, thanks to Gordon Thompson for his enthusiasm and dedication.

Contents

I. Topography

II. Interiors

III. Splitting space

Notes

About the author

I

Topography

Rain, back road

It is first of all belated, measured
a wet-fingered tally
on a nub of hill

then a Mandelbrot set
expanding on your forehead
Kleenexed away.

A goateed climatologist says
the planet has never gained
nor lost one drop—

each watery digit
a balance of payments
between heaven and earth.

Now implausible sheets
bed down dust
with an air of the profligate

and later, the day drilled
with the strange octaves
of birds

you say, as your dog steps
through theories of puddles
To drown well is art.

Topography

The fox you once saw
brushtailing into dusk
is back again.
At 3am I woke
to an animal wail
scoring the night.
Today I walk the drive,
the bony paddocks,
and find a sheep strewn
along the gully,
gutted mattress of a former self.
Crows circle the unsprung torso,
a blue wren pecks at shit.
I let the sheep trail drive me
further down the paddock,
knowing the neat vines opposite
have discipline I lack.
The canola
is fitful, shutting down
for half a year before its furious
yellow electrifies the fence.
Flowering gums
are manufacturing magenta,
along the drive
agapanthus nod and chant
We can do this. We can do this.
The old peppercorn says nothing.

Sometimes I sit by the shed
with its memory of horses
and machines we can't name.
The hill opposite raises
a tired spine,
fruit fall to the ground
soft as rabbit droppings.
A neighbour once told us
the sheep are for slaughter,
your dog straining at the lead.
Now a storm climbs over the hill.
Before it tears up clouds
the birds go crazy.

Introduced

Rats

We swept away shit
gathered in corners
like wild rice.
Fed them greens
shaken from a box
to stop the 3am whittling
of joists behind walls.
The worst was the litter
with its half-dead.
I buried them one
by one in the neighbour's paddock.
No matter how deep,
in the night
something dug them up.

Canola

There, suddenly perfect,
as if sprayed from a can.
More brilliant than a tub
of margarine, fitter than ever
since a pre-season
in the lab.

I love that blazing paddock,
treeless, with a two-storey stuck
in the middle, a kind of big
mid-American import.

Sheep

Pleading with day,
by night they chew
through our sleep.
Suckle, butt heads.
Mount. Break, again,
the pump at the trough.
You once freed one
from barbed wire
and it hurtled blindly
back into the fence.
Sometimes we stare at each other,
mutually unfathomable.
Their trails have hoof-like logic,
ramming the earth,
but often the greenest grass
is elsewhere.
Philip K. Dick's were electric.
Here's one lining the creek bed
unplugged by a fox.

Llamas

Platypus of the paddock,
kitted with necks
borrowed from giraffes,
their eyes do effortless 360s
like a bird's.
The brown one you call
Pie Face for the whip of cream
on its chocolate head

8

watches, a faggot
of boxthorn shackled to its hind.
Sounds its one-note whinny
like a truck in reverse.

Foxes

In the middle
of a ploughed paddock
a cub in the sun
scratching, our dog
delirious on the chain. Later
you played shepherd
and spooked one stalking
the flock. More often
we see them flung
on the shoulder
of a newly widened road,
accessorising
progress.

Hares

Before dusk is their time,
vellum antennae making a run for it.
Their droppings collect
like carefully gathered seed,
the land sown with hollows.
Yesterday one lay
beside the house,
pupils alive with flies.
It had taken bait

and suddenly we understood
the thumping in the night.

Bees

Not the native kind,
they installed themselves between loft floor
and ceiling boards.
The backyard became a contest
and the burly man was sent for.
We had heard of gentle smokings,
like those of a peace pipe.
Instead, a cube of pyrethrum,
cans of home brand spray.
Believe me, he said,
it's best. Sobbing, you went to bed.
I made him tea with four sugars
until the fury died.
Later we swept bodies,
removed the strange cumulus
of hive. It was like something
from a sci-fi. White, alien,
beautiful.

Tin shed

Someone squeezes
a mop out
in the sky;
we get
the scratchy bits
between tracks
on an old LP.

At night
a drum kit
for possums
or a birch
playing snares.

Now when the sun comes
you can hear God
leaning and expanding
on the roof.

Autumn

This is the fag end,
the faked ardour
of trees making fire
in their branches,
the chimney
on its first joint
of term,
the mirror plant
indifferent
above the octopus
of hose.

The light is thin,
the air smoggy
with confessions;
she hangs washing—
clippings for the neighbours
to read.

The birch clutches at summer
not wanting to let go
and from the clothes line
our shirts, dumbstruck,
throw out their arms.

Night train

A campaign of adjustment in tight seats
before you are pitched into darkness.
You think, dreamily, of Pasternak
but the woman opposite
is more *Blade Runner* than *Dr Zhivago*.
The carriage sashays and groans,
freeway lights arc
and you pass the outer rings of suburban Saturn,
the depopulated moons of stations.
Pods of luggage drip from racks,
the passengers are in suspended animation.
Upon reflection, the dark windows clone you.
Outside, the foggy anachronism
of steam, a raised flame—
refineries manufacturing industrial gothic.
The carriage follows a line
drawn beneath the You Yangs,
then the lights again, banking
in take-off.

Entering Geelong, as if you've clicked
Start slideshow, you see chain stores,
shopping plazas, empty car yards.
The hospital you were born in.
The school where you were clapped
and buggered, the church
where you begged forgiveness.
Your whole life.

Continental

Window shutters fold night away,
a woman walks her dachshund
on the sunny side of the street
and somewhere a church bell.
You pick red geraniums
from balcony pots (even car horns
sound different here), push
the rose of a shower
to my face.

Breakfast comes with forks
and syllables from the next table,
slivers of meat and knives
that torture cheese from pygmy packets.

The lift doors rattle in the foyer
and a concierge holds them
like a stagehand.
We post our room key
to a pigeon hole
but where did you learn
your beds bounce in a dozen tongues?

Outside the sun distils last night's wetness
and you have read somewhere
of cobblestones sculpted by men in chains.
Mannequins clad in dacron
blockade shop windows.
I open a map
and you turn it upside down.

Jaguar XJ 4.2, 1979

Something of the fox
and of the cat—
discreet and russet,
an outsider lying low.
Named after an African animal
by a former colonial power,
beneath its long bonnet
a snake pit of hoses
given to hissing
on hot summer days.
The interior a frayed glove
with leather seats well-thumbed
and smelling of neglected libraries.
Dash of walnut sans airbag
holding a kernel of the old country.

A predator like any feline
best kept in at night,
the wide stance of its carbon paw print
makes it the natural enemy
of the natural world.
Yet it has a memory of northern forests,
yearnings to search out old shires.
You can imagine a fondness
for Keats, Ted Hughes,
scarlet runners and poached artichokes.
Pre-glasnost maps of Europe.
It watches repeats of *The Avengers* on pay TV,
cashmere rug thrown over its boot.
Votes radical Tory and dreams of being driven

by Roger Moore. Thinks Miles Davis
should have stayed away from keyboards.
Calculates in imperial.

In Melbourne's fist of traffic
it is outmanoeuvred by SUVs,
shrugged off by Korean hatchbacks.
Turning the wheel to lock
earns a whine of protest
from the wide circle of its heart.
But on blonded peninsulas,
Sheffield six cylinders purring,
it leans into the road.
Hoovers past thin pastures, cattle yards,
manure at a dollar a bag.

As Anglophile fogs unfurl
across drought-stripped paddocks,
cells of coastal cancer divide
on metal skin.

Corio Bay

Face north where the You Yangs
rise like humps on a Photoshop loch,

a pelican jumbos over the bay
and three cargo ships convene—

there always seems to be one
from Panama.

On the eastern side men
extend the gardens with tip-truck and grader

while a tanned surveyor, shirtless,
calibrates the shifting earth.

Measuring him up, you
twist your ankle on a pine cone.

Saline solution

Salt and water become the ocean.
It's an alchemy like want and consent
yet still we can't discern
the quality of blue
or the rip in the heart.

There is longing, we know,
but build a bridge of sand
and see how far you get
while behind our backs
the sea shuffles its cards.
Beyond the pier
a yacht club's dry dock
is a bookcase for boats
as if the ways of water
can be catalogued.
Every buoy floats
its one hilarious trick before you.

This mast might be a pencil
underlining the sky
or a name. The afternoon
stretches its long body
on the shoreline, the sun
swooping the horizon
until deckchairs shut their mouths,
dusk brings its dun blanket to port
and there is nothing more to say.

Channel lights angling to be stars
blink with the rollout of night.
And when we have gone,
restless waves
will trample our sandy dedications
and mutter their way to shore,
dream of their own
half-won loves
and kick in their sleep.

Back beach, Point Lonsdale

for AFJ

It's summer and there's your dog
Hollywood
digging her way to Shanghai
her mane the colour of sun
the cuttlefish so many bleached
and meatless bones around her.
A tanker arcs the lighthouse
ghosting a route to China
or Panama, or a dock in Tuvalu
the pilot boat a brief haunting
to starboard.
It could be the eighteenth century
you say, *except for those cranes*
almost canons pistolling to port.
But here the sea barrels surfers
between peak and trough
the sand making small gifts
of pipi shells and seaweed
and for Hollywood, as you say
more rock pools than she can eat.
The wind rises and your chest
still in its bronchial wake
will soon return
to those eighteenth century
orchestrations, tossing you for hours
on the surface of sleep—
a dyspnoeic percussion
like the day's last waves

as they lick the rock pools.
Now the dog spins by
in happy sandy camouflage
eyes glassy, blind
to the deep thoughts of ships
the cargoes of fossil fuel
schools of fish twisting
beneath a hull.

Queenscliff–Sorrento ferry

Out here a dark tin foil unwraps
the home town's confidences
as a single strip of sun
makes an empty mall of a dolphinless sea

and with one long, languid step we are thrust
toward Sorrento, inviolable
in its all-weather whiteness,
its occidental logic and unimpeachable veneer

until the man beside me stands
and leaves an apple turnover crust
like a scallop shell
abandoned on his seat

while the crowd shuffles to walkways and
the water bright blue in happy turmoil
harangues the docking ferry, its fleet of cars a breed
of land-loving children greedy for shore

and then there's you … your crossed arms,
flat-foot patience, hair mission black
mid-point on the pier as the sun, refuelled,
makes me squint to see.

Light

There it is again, the world
turning over in bed.

The first magpie
undoes the dark, the dog

wet-noses our sleep
craving the back door.

The huntsman leaves off
its meditation on wall fixtures,

the clock radio squares time
and makes a number.

This is what some call
the stark reality of day.

The pole-vault sun
measures its stride

wall tile by wall tile
renames the streets,

spray-paints canola
across paddock floors.

Roadworkers commence
a ritual with witches hats—

flies arrive and spellbind
their flailing hands.

A cloud, blind grifter,
seeks the roof top, the dog's bowl.

A plane comes and tells us
of the bigness of things.

Callahans Lane

for AFJ

We plant the station wagon near the church
now a weekender for a German, Fritz,
and what the agent had murmured,
with a pause, was his younger partner. Our feet
become small outbursts on unsealed road.
After 200 metres, Sunday traffic is a memory.
Sheep stare, drifts of cumulus on barbed wire.
A bull all chest. And weirdly, those apple trees.

We cross a channel—the water, the long dry grass,
the dream of snakes too much for the dog,
mad kite on a lead. Stubbly paddocks,
shedding stretching the end of the road.
Aspect, the agent had said. *Listen*, you said.
Then the silence, time pegged out
with a crow call, stutters of small birds,
cattle with storybook questions.
Just one crow, you said. *Bad luck.*
We return to the car, drive back past the church
to glimpse Fritz and partner, not so young,
dismounting their VW. Past the house
we won't buy, the ageing vendor
who served cordial and told of the wife who left,
the children he never saw.

Day recoils and you fold maps,
the dog nails herself to the car floor.
In the rear vision starlings

picket a telephone line.
We note the modes of agency—
what was tendered, what trucked away—
and the road swallows itself.

II

Interiors

Noise

Twitterers, skeletal birds
on the wrong side of the perch, these
wire coat-hangers transmit their anxious thoughts
when I open the wardrobe door.
No jackhammers of the aviary,
still they manage 331.5 metres per second
of nervous tweeter through air
as if recalling a prehistoric explosion.
As if readying for flight.

Noise like that is soft and smells
of mothballs. But noise smells also
of burnt rubber and freshly cut steel. It sets
concrete dust in your nostrils and
headphones on teenagers making their way
to school. A DJ says he makes music
with 174 beats a minute. Noise like that
can put the lights down low
in your neighbour's house
and turn the lights on full in your own.

Noise is fluorescent yellow, electric orange
and alarm bell red. It is licorice allsorts.
It is the green line on a cardiac monitor.
Then there is white noise. Like white light
when all the colours become one.
Noise like that is quiet. The colour
of bleach, the colour of death, the colour
of 20,000 tones stripping away.

Quiet can be black too. The colour
of absolute silence. The dial tone
before the Big Bang.

My wardrobe will now consist of black and white.
Like an old-time nun or priest
I'll pass my days in silent prayer
embryoed in rhythms of monotone chant.
Sometimes I want my words ironed flat,
the soundwaves in space a waveless sea.
I want the universe to smell of starch again.

Proposition

You walked in, smooth as
liquid soap in a good hotel
and the breath of European dominions
opened with your coat.

Your lipstick held its nerve
while you revealed the choice line
of charms you deal in.
Look at this, you said

it's a favourite of mine.
It can be our talisman
a happy omen for all the sweet surrenders
we have hungered for in silence.

But my wants were basic.
I took it straight though I did appreciate
the side dish offered by the staff
attentive yet never intrusive.

Later there was a red coupé
a business plan destined to stay in black
the pledge to not become
an invoice arriving with the post.

Believe me, you said
my credit is good here—
your swipe-card prospects
my counterfeit smile.

Sonnet

The hills arrived and I kept driving.
With every civic car park this theory
Of joint tenancy grew more abstract.
There were shared passwords
And beds unmade with abandon,
But I didn't want to ruin
Our argument with the past.
Citing road kill would be callow
So I sent back cards
Left blank for your thoughts.
I counted ructions
And the miles between them.
Where the road withered
Lay a Switzerland of the heart.

Elementary physics

Last week I heard you have a PA
and it seemed to me you'd shattered
an invisible ceiling
while I was left below, staring up
shards of glass
snowing my hair and eyes.
I made my way
to the Bulldog Café for a toasted
ham and cheddar cheese sandwich
and that night dreamt of swipe-card doorways
your unimpeachable smile, a thousand casual
scorings. Pitch-forked awake, I rose
and sat in a chair in need of re-upholstery.
On the kitchen wall
two flies fucked while I considered
new ways of behaving badly.
It was as if you with your secret mark of Zorro
had cut to cartilage and bone
and with a barely explicable pain
I recalled your too-short legs rising
to just the right height, and how, dancing
you found the perfect centre of gravity.

Plot

You do the table plan and round up night.
I'll prepare toothpicks and dig
till there's a dark space underneath the house.

We'll need an unflinching gaze
an eye for the future
and every last drop of disinfectant.

It is not difficult to articulate
the anatomy of pain, every syllable
arching its back.

There is movement and there is stillness.
It's almost a reckoning of love
but I just can't count the ways.

These cuticles so white as if
we all wear rubber gloves
while the body performs its own recalculations.

With our answers sealed in plastic
this act binds us
more than love's tight fist.

Blood plums

We collect mail, and the years pass
Dark plums swamp the neighbour's tree
Vampires in the shed she has no key for
Then the starlings, the driveway paved with bloodied stones

Dark plums swamp the neighbour's tree
I found this black box at the end of the garden
Then the starlings, the driveway paved with bloodied stones
The rooms of that house never seeing sun

I found this black box at the end of the garden
By the side fence where a tricycle rusts
The rooms of that house never seeing sun
At night he fed her fear spoonful by spoonful

By the side fence where a tricycle rusts
These white plastic beads like somebody's childhood
At night he fed her fear spoonful by spoonful
One day I saw her mouth open and silent

These white plastic beads like somebody's childhood
Vampires in the shed she has no key for
One day I saw her mouth open and silent
We collect mail, and the years pass

The vexing

How dark he was.
He walked with his back hunched,
head lowered to inches above his toes.
As if he feared cavities,
anonymity.
That black dog,
stopping at every fence post.

He twitched. He was languid. At night
his bed clothes grew perturbed.
We sensed his not-quite-right
freedom from hunger.
As if he preferred worms,
a no-name soup. A watery grave.

He let his pen do the squirming.
But the paper grew wider,
emptier than the sea.

Much better like this.
Eating focaccia and waving
our mothers an acquiescent goodbye.
The past exits the back door
where pot plants do their time.
Next door a television
talks to the walls.

Interiors (goodbye Alanis)

This brunette hallway
a skin of carpet / recalling our footsteps
its whisper weaker each day / where the
tops of skirting boards arrest the fall of dust.

You said you can think of a number
that no-one else has
if it is big enough / there are more books
on shelves than can be read
only push-button phones
have redial / and maybe that's ironic.

Beneath this bed / one shoe
ready to rush the door
somewhere in a laundry basket
the usual crowd / wearing yesterday's bruises
and the debt collector of your heart.

I would like to see you / though
beyond the window only
the neighbour's kelpie cross yawns
at the sun / ticks off one more runaway car
in which a woman laughs
more desperately than she needs to.

And don't picture frames offer their own
sense of proportion above
a not-quite-flat mantelpiece / the
steady, unbroken breath of a gas heater
its hot blue flame.

Small things that lie ahead

A car passes and your heartbeat
trips through the door and walks out again.
The sun polishes hard surfaces,
every shadow is solid and still.
The microwave clock marks time.

Outside, the morning glory guards the window,
knowing it has gone too far.
Beyond, deep in the blue,
a flock of birds gathers itself,
moves into the window frame
and out of it.

Later the rain will press low and hard,
rouse the tin roof,
scribble its bullet-point fears.

Subsequently

A slow siren
called from far off
and that was one of us.
Then just the soft,
steady ruminations of the fridge.

Sometimes I tell myself
unoccupied space
can be a good thing:
a notepad with unbroken blue lines,
the concrete expansion of a suburb,
a window.

Today the wall clock calls its name
three thousand six hundred times an hour.
I count the small silences.

On reflection

Today you're on celluloid
or at least parked
at the very next table;
a chin in relief,
one hand skirting
a cup on a saucer
and almost beyond reach
chopsticks of sugar
inside a glass,
the salt like talc,
the ground brown pepper
so fine and smooth
it could be art
in a bottle.

Blooming

after Robyn Stacey, Waratah, *lenticular photograph, 2003*

A rose perhaps with issues
but up close you lose perspective.

It's the same with saying a word
too many times and suddenly you've forgotten
what *earth, stamen, light, desire* mean.

All too strange
or too familiar, we can't decide.

But this mouth explodes
or we think it does
and it speaks to us in tongues.

We don't always know the language
and sometimes it isn't subtle
yet it's an art of sorts
and we have one colour committed to memory.

A garment shrugged off,
a doorway with red light open then closed
then open again.

Wedding party

Be natural.
And from left
a child blows bubbles
for the video.

Everyone seems fit
to laugh.

Women in pink
hold men
in matching ties,
the bride
an empty purse.

Aunt Vera
stumped in a wheelchair.

The groom is invisible
but there is always another man
with ponytail and cummerbund
who leans to the side
chewing gum.

One of the bubbles
breaks in mid air.
Somewhere
a woman is in tears.

Suddenly

The ceiling lowers to build a bank of lights.
Like the set of *All the President's Men*,
a composition in fluoro framed
with performance indicators.
And I am calm, becalmed, totting
up my inbox as if one more cc'd email
might offer my last pass out.

Carpet spawns loose threads,
tendrils of grey zoo. An acrylic
grassland for pinstriped herds.
Beatings will continue until morale improves
our handler decrees. Shackled and impatient
we queue at his door. The photocopier
offers a full and accurate record.

A man known for meeting objectives
loaded like bullets on a page says
They're hungry. The hoarse whisperer
in the next cubicle says *Follow the money.*

I rig my screen with idiot stare.
Somewhere a director calls cut, and fires.

Five easy pieces

deliverance

a trout with three eyes
the factory pipe trickling
melodically

différence

left without a thought
The Essential Derrida
alone on a chair

naked lunch

a picnic on grass
bullants crazy with intent
my lack of control

living in the 70s

tonight on TV
the dwarf dressed in white
cried *Da plane! Da plane!*

cast away

oh no! you said
it's Tom Hanks, all hairy
on a raft!

Sunday

You asked me to touch you
from behind.
I did
and that was the end
of the market.

Brick

With your grim smile
and abstemious ways,
to some a template for solidity,
and I know you did the right thing
with that safe haven for pigs.

But it's your intransigence that gets me—
the chip-on-your-shoulder
doorstop quality, the ascetic,
the paperweight (don't you ever
lighten up?) for last week's news
where others are war torn
and you debris.

I've met your dumb siblings,
militants all,
each harder than a dog biscuit
and just as endearing.
I suggested ping pong
yet they remained unmoved
even if they did return the ball.

And you so orthodox, so starchy,
so … straight. There's a fence in China
made of your kind; pyramids
in Egypt, suburbs, nations
secure and languishing,
every one of them still
billeting the dead.

III

Splitting space

Blast

This word comes with an assignment.

Yesterday we read about a joyride,
someone's window of opportunity
too brilliant to ignore,
the silhouettes of passers-by
reflected in glass,
and at times, peering in,
we saw only ourselves.

It went straight to the heart,
all of us stirred and shaken
even this side of town,
the guilty exultation of blood pumping
faster and redder than it used to,
our skin crawling with dark wonder
and still the house wears postcards
of Kuta and Tomorrowland
and fridge magnets
collected in the post.

I saw you on the front page,
smiling, last summer's package holiday
reflected in your eyes,
an arranged marriage with the future before you;
ever the diplomat, it made me think
of coconut milk, a long glass, a path
swept free of leaves.
But the earth turns and the sun
shines in more than one sky

yet not everyone knows that more than history
is tattooed on the forehead,
that in mountains the night kills quickly.
Note how high-rises shadow, effortlessly,
dogs with mange in the laneway;
somewhere we can't see
a credit card whispers
I want you.

The small are sometimes strong
and bring their own exhilarations.
Now, here is my opening.

Elegy

1.

murmurings of war—
in an unmarked sky a jet
dreams new script

*

on the powerline
crows collecting like small deaths
and then a wingbeat

*

already wearing black
two million office workers
prepare themselves

*

rumours from the city—
we check the basement, our phones
and still no answer

*

something upon us
the spotlight of terror
a new kind of love

*

empty house
the leaves, the man with his past
the earth rushing up

*

blue lights, sirens
the urban constellations
of alarm

*

frame by frame
nights stretched out on plasma
flowers on footpaths

*

last night on TV
he said, *we will find them*
we will find them

2.

turning from her desk
a doctor opens her hands
and the clocks change hour

*

all through summer
vans with lights on during day
ferry the silent

*

the return home—
after filling up our cars
we count boxes

*

a short speech of road
where the blackbird strings up worms
plaques buttoning earth

*

and these found objects—
a toothbrush, a gas bill
the neat bed

*

in today's paper
ringed with coffee stains
this receipt of you

Ash Wednesday

Fold up the angel wings,
bring out sackcloth,
have the hired help
compost the flowers.
Make *pallor* a word
for ashen faces
and when shadows take root
beneath our eyes
we'll see the future
in print already.

Grave blessings but
see how schoolchildren enjoy
the mask of dark brows.
We all know the small rapture
of abstinence and desire.

On the edge of town
those trees that gestured
grandly last year
now rumour with fire.

Morning. The rainless clouds.
The red and purple sky.

Duck season

Flying
where the Custard Cream
of sun was dunked.

The sky teal
and storybook purple
where they fly from.

Flying to the window
of a Chinese take-away
on the other side of town.

Wings working overtime,
always
more of them coming.

Jemima sporting
blue bonnet and shawl,
but someone from here
got shot.

That must be her
behind the others,
flying alone
and weighted with onions.

Come be my quilt
or my quill.

Pookie believes in Santa Claus

Here's our man
decked out in red
and mounted on a surfboard.

Everyone is wearing new T-shirts
and your strung-up cards
make our fireplaces smile
in summer.

The big bird more than we can eat,
the bonbons a reliable bad joke.
Beneath the TV
the plastic infant looks composed
for a refugee.

Santa, pack your car,
the roads will soon be heavy with traffic.

Burying Mary

We all wear sunglasses as if blinded by a final light.

Here are the men in black,
square as a box,
shouldering the blunt bow,
below them the cut earth a glittering
net of dropped pearls
or decommissioned, unstrung stars.

Note the fingernails sanded clean,
cheeks polished to bear
the dusty kisses of aunts.
Heads listing, theatrically,
towards the vortex.

The priest flicks water. Beads of it
glimmer on our shoes.

At the threshold we find elbows to grasp,
but coming from the suburbs
none of us are sure what we see.

Yellow brick road

Her card parties, parish fundraisers
and the stretch of blue cellophane
on the black-and-white TV
something special.

We got the lay-down misère
on old age, heard the nagging rattle
of her stick on floorboards, of rosary beads,
her shallowing breath.

She once called me Dorothy,
muddling me
with a Kansas farm girl
taken with the wind.

So slowly she now travels Ormond Road
with headlights on at noon.
Confused perhaps by the journey
or the destination.

Six feet of separation

He had once been a gardener
and when I visited
in a moment of semantic acumen
he called his wheelchair
a wheelbarrow.

Across the road
the earth has been turned
and it is patient, deliberate,
without words.

This new space

Last night we watered a toothbrush
so the bristles wouldn't die.
Refreshed the memory folds
of a black umbrella.

I've seen the rooms
inside a glove
moulded by a hand not there.

Night has a language all its own.
They say hearing is the last thing to go.

The big wave

Here we find evidence of sand reallocated.
Their clothing will be nearby
half-swallowed by desert.

Look, a gull elbows horizons
into unknown latitudes.

Now she turns and draws hair
over shoulders that seem wider than his.

See their eyes following, almost swooping (if we take some licence),
recognition taking wing.

He feels seaweed desperate at his ankle.

Note the sea at this penultimate moment is speechless,
its one thought roaming between thigh and neck.

Plunge

An expensive trick with mirrors
or they are right
who say glass is liquid.
Perhaps the underworld is cool and turquoise
maybe the sky upside down
where we start flying.

This air pasty enough to stroke
it folds blankets in our ears
and everything reeks of blue.
I see the daytime moon of your face
your body a cloud evolving.

Our fall is buoyant and we now know for sure
that heaven has confines I nearly
broke my elbow on them.

Sometimes it feels we don't belong:
here, lend me your gas mask.

Carousel

The music, the giddiness; to remember with a mirror
The locals smiling and fettered
The space undulating
Townsfolk saying you'd come back again

The locals smiling and fettered
You so happy you could have been in orbit
Townsfolk saying you'd come back again
Did it look like we were your stars?

You so happy you could have been in orbit
That dark side, lost to our sight
Did it look like we were your stars?
You ask the question and each reply is the same

That dark side, lost to our sight
A journey, or the end of one
You ask the question and each reply is the same
The planets sure in their step

A journey, or the end of one
The space undulating
The planets sure in their step
The music, the giddiness; to remember with a mirror

Crossing

Traveston, Queensland, 9 June 1925

The vast tablets of light
above our heads
signalled *a way forward*.

Our carriage wielded its penchant
for the straight and narrow.
A sense of being acted upon.

We considered the data:
bridges signed by the underworld,
bells tolling,
crosses angled
to be borne by saviours.

But we were sleeping
and in the slow miracle of curve
we dreamt of a clerk's office, a foundry.
A milliner's, a beach.

Things happen. A strange
stuttering of carriage.
A riff of metal
and wood.
Our unexpected heft
into that derailed night.

Wingless, we drew
a downward arc through sky.

There was a moment
of stillness, as if our capsule
might forever split space.
I remember the slow dislodgement
of a feeding bottle,
a woman's hat taking leave.

Before the new configuration
of tissue and kindling,
before our bodies embossed earth,
I heard a whirring of air.
A howl. A child's brief,
disembodied cry.

The face

After the womb, after your wailing entrée
you fixed on this—

this rolling membrane with more muscles
than a foot, softer than an elbow

its perpetual *hello how ru?!*
more telling than asking.

And you rose and faced the day
the sun pulling out

with the morning train—
a whistle blew and you logged on

and everywhere met that long chicane of features
worked in vellum, bone and pixel

seven billion ways
of travelling with the Other

and counting, each an anthology
of anticipation, rapture and *guilt about the past*

a précis
of call and response.

Now you're sorry Borges did not construe
a library of all possible faces

where you would fall through space
reading furrowed lines in past and future tense

of how each beautiful self
falls through cracks

so that we and all our effects arrive on schedule
not knowing the coming after.

Notes

'Suddenly': '*They're hungry*' and '*Follow the money*' are taken from the Alan J. Pakula film *All the President's Men*, Warner Bros., 1976, which in turn was based on the book by Carl Bernstein and Bob Woodward, Simon & Schuster, New York, 1974.

'Duck season' draws in part from Beatrix Potter's *The Tale of Jemima Puddleduck*, Frederick Warne & Co., London, 1908.

'Pookie believes in Santa Claus' derives its title from the children's book of the same name by Ivy L. Wallace, Collins, London, 1953.

'Yellow brick road': Ormond Road borders the southern side of the Geelong Eastern Cemetery.

'Crossing': Shortly before 2am on 9 June 1925, at Traveston, near Gympie, Queensland, the luggage van of the Rockhampton Mail train derailed. After travelling a further 2.4km, the van plunged over the side of the 96 Mile Bridge, taking with it two carriages. Nine people died, 55 were injured.

About the author

Anthony Lynch lives on the Bellarine Peninsula where he writes poetry, fiction and reviews. His work has appeared in *The Age*, *Best Australian Poems*, *Island* and *Southerly*, and been read on ABC Radio National. His short story collection *Redfin* (Arcadia) was shortlisted for the Queensland Premier's Literary Awards. He is publisher at the independent publishing house Whitmore Press and an editor at Deakin University.